F

Fearful- Avoidant in Love
How Understanding the Four Main Styles of Attachment Can Impact Your Relationship

JOHANNA SPARROW

Johanna Sparrow

Fearful-Avoidant in Love

Smashwords Edition

Fearful-Avoidant in Love Revised© 2018 Johanna Sparrow All rights reserved.
WWW.JOHANNASPARROW.COM
www.10minuterelationshipadvicewithjohannasparrow.com

Edited By: H e a t h e r P e n d l e y
www.pendleysproediting.com Cover design: www.milagraphicartist.com

Johanna Sparrow

Fearful- Avoidant in Love
How Understanding the Four Main Styles of Attachment Can Impact Your Relationship

Fearful-Avoidant in Love

Johanna Sparrow

CONTENTS

Introduction

Who's Loving the Fearful- Avoidant Partner?

No One Wants the Dismissive-Avoidant Partner

Leaving the Anxious-Preoccupied Partner Behind

In Search of the Secure Partner

Change Your Attachment Style

Attachment Styles

What Do You Want from Me?

Change Your Attitude

How Attachment Styles Can Affect Your Relationship

Conclusion

INTRODUCTION

You've been playing games in your relationship for far too long and it's about to cost you everything you want, love. If you don't pull it together and get a grip, you will be by yourself in the coming months and this you know. Your commitment phobic behavior is brighter than a neon sign and your partner is not the only one who sees it.

You've been dating the same person off and on for the past five years. You know everything about them. Every few months, your breaking-up, and getting back together as if nothing happened. Your make-up moments are exciting. But lately, you've been living for those make-up moments more than the actual relationship. You feel helpless if not loss in your next move, but you tell yourself it will get better. If you don't pull it together soon and stop the games, breakups will be the high-lite of your relationship.

As soon as someone gets close to you, you are pushing them away if not out the door. You don't trust them, but you want a relationship with them anyway. You don't want to be left behind or thrown away like a piece of garbage. Loving you can cause anger, distraction and distance what I like to call, (ADD), but it's how someone like you feels loved. This passive aggressive behavior keeps your partner trying to figure you out daily, but they never will. You switch up on them every chance you get never allowing them to know your next move. You have a parade of charades that'll drive anybody loving you crazy if not to drinking. You push the right buttons at the right time than take the backseat approach when things get too hot I see what you're doing, you're so afraid of being alone and not wanted or loved that you manufacture drama in order to keep things spiced up in your relationship.

You aren't fooling anyone around here. You see that push and pull tug of war you are pulling in your relationship baby is all about control.

You taking this don't leave me love thing too damn far. Something about them needing you frightens the hack out of you and red flags are what get you in your head. You are not about to get your heart broken without taken a few along the way. Why so scared? You want this love or not? If you aren't holding them tight, you're barely holding them at all. Your crazy ways got them confuse. You depend on your partner like your lifeline yet play that don't care

Fearful-Avoidant in Love

attitude when you know you do. Afraid of rejection, abandonment and intimacy should be your name, but who cares you're in love. You put up with the foolishness because you don't think you can get better all while telling yourself you can. Forget trusting your partner, you trust no one. You challenge everything others say to you and see yourself as less than those around you. You walk a thin line between loving and hating yourself. Sure, that may work for some, but I know who you are. I know your low self-esteem plays a major role in how you view yourself in your relationship and from where I'm standing, not good at all.

You tend to wear your feelings on your sleeve for all to see while swearing up and down nothing bothers you. You can become needy, clingy and a cry baby at the drop of a hat, which makes your partner feel pressure to stay with you.

At times you back down when you think you will lose them for good, but that's the game you've always played. You are a mess and the wheels in your head keep on turning. You would not be alone because finding love is too damn hard. Once someone loves you, you hold on for life. You have no problems showing your feelings, but be aware it will cost your partner later on.

Fearful-Avoidant in Love

You'll open book and many of your pages have been torn out. You care what others say about you and don't know your own worth. Why so disconnected? The biggest question of them all is, why are you so fearful of love? So often, you are overacting to everything around you. It's no wonder your relationships fall apart. Could it be, you don't understand love?

This was the conversation a man had with himself before going into the house. "I can't ever seem to get this love thing right," he says. "Never one for playing the role of the fool for anyone. I just can't lose this person in my life. I may never find another like them. Who else would love me? This is the best I can do.

He walks in the house, kisses his woman and grabs a cold beer out the fridge. "What you've been up to?" his girlfriend's say. "Working hard and making you happy," he replied. And as she leans in to kiss him on the lips, he jumps out of his seat. Shocked, by his sudden movement she pulls away. The more she pulls away the safer he feels within his relationship. He's not giving up, but she is. He will do all he can to convince her that she's loved, even as far as tattooing her name across his chest. Keeping her confused about the relationship is the game he plays. The more he makes her think that something is wrong the harder she works for his love.

Before going to bed he lights candles for a romantic evening, his behavior must have frightened her. Winning her back is all he thinks about. He walks up to her with a half open shirt and a fresh tattoo across his chest that reads, "Your Fearful-Avoidant in love." This small act of love brings them closer than they've ever been. Loving in fear is how they live it's as simple as that. The truth is, fearful avoidant is one of four attachment styles that slowly sucks the life out of a relationship. Fearful of rejection and abandonment, a person with the fearful-avoidant attachment style is passive aggressive and has a hard time seeing their own worth. They question why you love them or want to be with them every chance they get. Even if they care about you, you will be confused.

The fuss behind the attachment styles as it relates to adult relationships, goes back to childhood and how you viewed the people close to you and how you formed attachments during that period. If your needs weren't met by your parents when you were a child and you sought their attention, chances are that you do the same thing in your adult relationships. This attachment style is a mixed bag of emotions that won't allow you to be hurt and causes you to go out of your way to draw first blood if you have to.

After learning so much about attachment styles from family and friends and from within my own relationship, it was only fitting for me to share my perspective on the four attachment styles so that you can better understand your relationship and your partner's needs. This book focuses on all of the attachment styles, but highlights the fearful-avoidant attachment style partner at it's best.

WHO'S LOVING THE FEARFUL-AVOIDANT PARTNER?

Loving the fearful-avoidant partner is like waking up every day on the wrong side of the bed. Someone is afraid to love. Someone is afraid to let go when things are bad. The push and pull tugging back and forward is what keeps them grounded if not holding on for dear life. They've got you wrapped around their little finger and not letting you go. Inside you may be screaming for a breakup, but afraid it will cause you to lose out on love later on if not forever. You need

Fearful-Avoidant in Love

to know they aren't going to just up and leave you alone. You need to know that they love you just as much as you love them. You need to know that your heart is in a safe place when it comes to loving them. Your military tactics keeps you up in your head when you don't get the answers you seek. Playing games with their heart and mind is how you love.

This kind of love is dangerous. On one end you got it together, but as soon as things feel right, you question everything including the air they breathe. Why can't you just relax and go with the flow of things? Why can't you love yourself more?

You can't because you stay in your head questioning everything they do. If you aren't looking to be alone, you are sure pushing the envelope in it's direction. You have more fears about loving your partner than the average person and struggle with enjoying yourself around them. Could it be you feel you don't deserve love? Why think this way and expect a loving relationship in the process? Didn't anyone ever tell you loving in fear is dangerous.

Your fear to love and open your heart every day slowly drains the very life out of your partner if not the relationship. Your crazy way of thinking is killing the very essence of everything you desire. Your words are like a

Fearful-Avoidant in Love

poisonous brew. But still you ask the same damn question daily. Why did you pick me? Why do you love me? As if you don't know already? You are worthy of love when you are not in your head or questioning things. When you are not operating in a state of fear, you are the coolest person to be with. Your sense of humor is on point and keeps your partner laughing. And that confidence is engaging making you hard to resist. Who wouldn't want someone like you? Why are you shocked that love wants you? Why so hard on yourself? Why people fall in love with someone who expects the worse is beyond me.

They wear the badge commitment- phobe across their chest. They make it hard for you to love them mainly because they feel they aren't deserving of your love. If you are in a relationship with the fearful- avoidant partner realize everything you tell them is taken as a lie. Your arguments are overrated and taken to the extreme because they see it as the relationship not working. What is normal when it comes to expressing one's feelings for the fearful-avoidant partner is terrifying.

They fear abandonment and rejection. They even seek to make you happy putting aside their own happiness to keep you in the relationship. They are far from crazy and uses their mixed-up ways to distract you from their fear. You can easily be on the receiving end of such a relationship. At times you may feel as if your partner is interrogating you. Rest assure that's the fearful-avoidant style of love.

This type of person is afraid of being alone. Have you been confused in your relationship? Are you asking for forgiveness for something you didn't say or do? That's the fearful-avoidant style at work. This push and pull, up and down fight for control is the workings of the fearful-avoidant partner. They are negative when it comes to love. They are known best for using past hurt as an excuse to be mean to you and anyone else they feel like mistreating. Holding a negative view of themselves and others is how they cope. It helps them avoid getting hurt. Overtime, you find yourself on a rollercoaster of emotional torments.

If this is the attachment style you're dealing with? Your partner may be viewing themselves in a negative way. This type of person can have a self-sabotaging attitude and getting close to them can be difficult. More than often this person feel love is not for them, so rejecting you is how they protect their heart.

Connecting on a deeper level may be difficult for them in the beginning. They've been hurt and don't want to be hurt again. If

Fearful-Avoidant in Love

you are with this type of person be prepared to maintain the relationship since their fearful of losing, you are always on their mind. A fearful-avoidant person seeks approval and validation from others. Changing their perspective on love won't be easy. Constantly seeking acceptance is what hurts the relationship ultimately ending it. When their partner puts in the effort to make them feel good, they struggle with intimate connections and fear of getting hurt, so they pull back. They struggle with initiating closeness and intimacy for fear of rejection. This type of person feels the need to protect themselves by having control over the relationship. Sure, you want to have a healthy relationship like the next person, but your fearful-avoidant person's mindset keeps them in a prison of fear.

Although you allow yourself to get into relationships with others, this attachment style struggles to move to the next level, which is emotional intimacy, and thus finds themselves uncomfortable letting others get close to them because rejection is a constant thought. This self-consciousness that people experience with this attachment style can lead to being dependent in relationships. The ugly truth is that fear isn't the only thing that someone with the fearful- avoidant attachment style goes through. Trust is another thing they struggle with, and they may have struggled with this throughout their entire life. In their minds, avoiding emotions is a way to stay safe from changes in a relationship.

Vulnerability is also an issue. Anything that calls for them to display affection forces them to shut down. They avoid conflict, so working out problems won't be easy. Once you're in a relationship with the fearful-avoidant attachment style partner, they tend to cycle in and out of insecurity. Finding a healthy balance with their feelings and trusting their partner, is very difficult for them. Wanting a relationship without putting in the work and time, is difficult and almost guarantees failure, but for this type of partner, it's normal. They see everything as their fault and fear the relationship ending.

Learn to give more of yourself, and over time you will see that trusting yourself and others is a more powerful state than being closed off and fearful.

NO ONE WANTS THE DISMISSIVE-AVOIDANT PARTNER

You've been thinking about ending the relationship, but thought about all of the sweat and tears you've put into it. Why quit now is what you tell yourself.

This relationship has it's own language and you'll not about to let anyone put you in a venerable state. You would cut them off before you allow that to happen. If your partner doesn't know where you stand when it comes to love and romance, you are not about to tell them nor show them the way.

Each man for him-or-herself is the approach you take and for good reason, you've been hurt more times than you would like. That take it or leave it attitude of yours is what keeps your partner attached to the hip. Something about your loving along with your laid-back attitude and dismissive approach is what they need. When they love hard, you can care less that's until you feel them pushing you away. Like falling out of your seat, you pick the pace up in the relationship quick, fast and in a hurry. You have no problems showing your partner you

Fearful-Avoidant in Love

don't care, but let the tables turn, you find the strength to save the relationship.
What you don't like is being left behind by anyone. If you aren't the one with the take it or leave it attitude, you can't handle it.

If your partner ever learns this, you would be in a world of trouble. Putting up a wall is your way of feeling safe, but that hasn't always worked for you. You've learn that loving anything too much can be painful, so you pull away from your partner from time to time in hopes that it confuses them or make them question your love.
You want love and know you are deserving of it, but you or your partner holds back

their feelings and it's enough to make you want to scream. Loving someone with the dismissive- avoidant attachment style isn't easy and can make you feel as if they are in a relationship all by themselves. Getting your partner to care about your feelings and show you more attention can feel like a job. When it comes to the dismissive avoidant attachment style, less is more. They have no problems flexing their independence in your face. Your partner has their guard up when it comes to loving you in the relationship and no matter how much you work to make them feel loved and safe, you won't get the love you need unless it's on their terms. You will have to keep up or cut them off it's just that simple.

And the more you seek for them to show you love, you get nothing but frustration. A dismissive-avoidant personality is all about control and plenty of it. Loving them feels more like a game than an actual relationship. If they ever decide to let you in, you find yourself putting up with more drama than you could want.

Can you truly love the dismissive avoidant partner? You are not the problem, if you are struggling with one if not many of the attachment styles and you two are never on the same page when it comes to attachment styles. If one of you aren't showing the dismissive- avoidant style the other the fearful avoidant style. The back and forth pushes your relationship to the limit and forces you or your partner to take a defensive approach when communicating. Having a broken heart is the last thing the dismissive avoidant partner wants. They have a me against the world mentality and the more you push to show them otherwise, the more you argue. Step back for a second and really look at what you are dealing with on a daily basis.

If you want this relationship to work, you have to do more than seek after their love. You have to be able to understand the way they think when it comes to giving their heart away. The dismissive-avoidant partner wants no more than to be loved, but struggle with showing their true feelings.

Learning what your partner needs is important to your relationship surviving. If you are struggling with loving your dismissive-avoidant partner it's because they have a difficult time trusting their heart to anyone, including you. Be patient and keep a positive outlook on your relationship. Know your partner wants to give you their heart, but don't want to bet hurt. Don't hold back your love, the more you love them and make time, they eventually come around. If you are dealing with one of the four attachment styles, balancing yourself is the key to being happy as well as understanding your partners fears.

If you're with someone that exemplifies this attachment style, you need to seek help through family counseling or coaching. Focus on things in the relationship that takes the stress off of you or your partner needs since giving love is where they tend to hold back. It isn't going to get any better. Your partner may be guarded with his-or-her feelings to let you in.

In time they will let down their guard. Keep in mind that your dismissive- avoidant partner is independent, self- sufficient, and has a take it or leave it mentality when it

Fearful-Avoidant in Love

comes to love or expressing his-or- her feelings. They've learned how to suppress the one thing they want, love in order to not get hurt. Making themselves vulnerable is how they feel they will get hurt in the relationship, so they don't take rejection or break-up well. Keeping their heads on straight through how much love and attention you receive from them is how they maintain control.

You will feel as if you are all alone in the relationship. Feeling neglected is or not loved is how most people feel in relationships with the dismissive-avoidant attachment style. Your relationship has more ups and downs than others and fighting to stay connected or not give up on your partner is what keeps you hanging on. If this is the case, you may need to seek advice on dealing with your emotions and feelings when it comes to your dismissive- avoidant partner.

The dismissive-avoidant is conflicted in his-or-her feelings when it comes to their partners needs and their desire for independence. They want both love and independence, but struggle to meet the needs of a loving relationship.

The dismissive-avoidant partner pushes you away if they feel you want more of a connection from them. They must overcome their trust issues before letting anyone in.

Below is a list of behaviors you may witness in a dismissive-avoidant partner:

- Keeps partner seeking attention.
- Uses distractions to keep from sharing their feelings with their partner.
- Shuts down during important conversations.
- Struggles to show love or express his-or-her feelings.
- Focuses on past issues.

- Push and pull. Push away when things are good, pull closer when things are bad.
- Refusal to commit but remains in a relationship.
- Reluctant to say, I love you.
- Looks to argue instead of working out their differences.
- Uses distractions as a way to control the relationship.

This type of attachment style makes having a successful relationship very difficult. If you are your partner needs extreme independence, this attachment style is the reason. You can change what's going on in your relationship once you discover what's happening. If you're in heavy conflict with your dismissive-avoidant partner, you can find balance by knowing the right things to do without adding any more trauma to an already painful situation.

Below is a list of how a dismissive avoidant can take control of their fears and allow themselves to experience real love:

- Focus on positive experiences within your relationship.

- Communicate your feelings without judgment.
- Confront your fears about rejection.
- Focus on finding security within yourself.
- Learn to recognize when you are allowing the dismissive avoidant attachment style to influence your behavior.
- Make your relationship priority.
- Turn away from negative thoughts and behaviors.

To the dismissive avoidant person, once you remove fear and open your heart, you will feel safe and happy in your relationship.

Fearful-Avoidant in Love

By focusing on intimacy, you will begin the process of making your relationship strong.

If you are not ready to give a 100 % in your relationship, you should let your partner know so they can move on. To the dismissive-avoidant, it's never too late to open your heart and share your feelings with the person you love. Even though there's no guarantee that you won't get hurt, you still deserve to love and be love. The more you reject the love that's offered to you, the unhappier you become, keeping you stuck in a cycle of fear and uncertainty. Never allow fear and negative thinking to take over your mind. Doing so can put you in an emotional state of mind.

You end up turning your back on those things that are important to you such as love. Give love a chance and know that you deserve love.

LEAVING THE ANXIOUS-PREOCCUPIED PARTNER BEHIND

You've been dealing with the push and pull in your relationship and find that your partner fears of loving you keep them at an emotional distance. Do they know how this makes you feel? If they don't make you priority your fear is that the relationship will be over. Your need for validation and approval is suffocating the life right out of your relationship.

If this is how you or your partner is acting blame it on the anxious-preoccupied attachment style. The constant need to feel loved by their partner is taking a toll on everything. Not feeding you the attention and validation you need creates a blender of emotions inside. For starters you're in a

mental game of wondering if you're worthy of love.

If different attachment styles are operating within your relationship, you may be finding it difficult to get a hold of your emotions. Who doesn't want to feel appreciated? But the anxious-preoccupied partner needs can be unrealistic. If you aren't getting what you want in your relationship you go into negative thinking that leads to you feeling your partner may not be as in love with you as you are with him-or-her. No matter how much time you make for them it's never enough for the anxious-preoccupied attachment style partner. It's their way or the highway.

Arguments become a daily or weekly routine in the relationship if you aren't giving them what they want, time. A healthy relationship does not struggle with intimacy or closeness, but that's the core issues when dealing with an anxious- preoccupied partner.

Your constant craving for their attention becomes the core problem in the relationship. Your partner may see you as always being needy and never satisfied. Learn how to go with the flow of the relationship. When you force things to happen it can cause a world wind of other issues you're not expecting.

Stop being selfish and learn how to be grateful with the time you have. Neglecting your partners needs will only keep your relationship unhealthy. You must learn to love yourself first and not look to anyone to make you happy. Take accountability of your actions and behaviors when it comes to your relationship. If you pick with your partner instead of talking to them about your feelings, you will end up in unnecessary arguments.

If you are loving someone out of fear it only forces, you to live in fear. The anxious-preoccupied partner puts undo pressure on an already fragile relationship.

Breathe, and take each day at a time when it comes to your relationship. The anxious-preoccupied attachment style as you know feels insecure. They struggle with low self-esteem and may put all of their focus on you meeting their needs. Since the anxious-preoccupied attachment style sees themselves in a negative light, they go out of their way to get what they want from their partners the most, attention, validation and approval.

Shifts in your relationship, good or bad, lets your partner know how to respond to you, since they're always evaluating the relationship and whether you care or not. If the anxious-preoccupied partner doesn't feel the connection with their partner, they may look outside the relationship to feed the need for affection or to make their partner jealous. During childhood, this type of a partner may have not received the amount of attention they wanted and needed from one or both parents, and as a result, they act out for attention.

Below is a list of how the anxious-preoccupied partner behaves in relationships:

- Feel anxious until they are around their partner.
- Keeping score by counting wrongdoings and never granting true forgiveness.
- Threatening to leave partner as a form of control.
- Always wants to stay in contact with partner via text, call, or email.

Because the anxious-preoccupied partner has a negative self-image and thinks everyone else is better than them, they fear disconnection from their partner. The longer you're in a relationship with an anxious-preoccupied partner, the more you'll find yourself babysitting their needs, which never seems to be enough. Their need for a strong relationship with closeness and validation is how they receive love, and if you don't give them constant attention, they're likely to act out in rage. If they feel that their relationship is in a crisis situation, they tend to want even more attention and affection.

Fearful-Avoidant in Love

The only way to work through difficult times with an anxious-preoccupied partner is by understanding their needs and being careful not activating their fears.

Can you imagine if you were an anxious-preoccupied partner that is in a relationship with a dismissive-avoidant partner? The truth is, I've seen this type of couple in my family and amongst my friends. Their daily struggle to get along is extremely difficult. While one seeks for closeness and intimacy, the other seeks independence. Sure, they have some good times together, but I've noticed that if one partner is insecure with self-esteem issues and the other has a positive self-image, it can make one partner feel like they aren't loved enough. It then becomes the constant focus of the anxious-preoccupied partner to seek and force love and validation from their dismissive-avoidant partner.

Living on edge is never a good thing in a relationship, just ask someone with the anxious-preoccupied attachment style. Having a partner who is just as fearful, that doesn't give a damn, or is insecure, makes each person have to work harder for love. Now you can see how easy it is to cause someone with this attachment style to feel unsure about themselves. The person with the anxious-preoccupied attachment style becomes upset easily and they constantly have the emotional need to be close to their partner. If we clearly look at this anxious-preoccupied attachment style and its deficiencies, we will come to understand the mindset of someone with this attachment style.

Below is a list of the thinking patterns of the anxious-preoccupied attachment style:

- Constantly thinks about their partner and has trouble staying focused on other things.

- Thinks of the positive qualities that they don't have.

- Constantly places partner on a pedestal while by putting themselves down and underestimating their own abilities.

- Needs to stay in contact with partner at all times.

- Believes this is the only love they will receive. "I don't think anyone would love me the way you do."

- Even when they're unhappy in a relationship, tells themselves that they won't find anyone better.

When this attachment style is met with love and attention, everything calms down and life goes back to normal. When this person's attachment needs go unfulfilled, things go from bad to worst and the anxious person's behavior spirals out of control. Protest-like behavior is seen when things aren't right in the relationship, and the couple fights and struggles to regain control by requiring that their needs be met. Analyzing the protest behavior with this attachment style is just as important as everything else in the relationship. Keeping the relationship unbalanced by refusing to connect or show affection, can cause damage over time.

Below is a list of protest behavior methods from the anxious-preoccupied attachment style:

- Excessive need to stay connected.
- Hostility.
- Keeping score of wrongdoing.
- Making partner feel jealous.
- Manipulation.
- Threatening to leave or end the relationship.

If this is something that resonates with you, understanding the needs of your attachment style can strengthen your relationship. When you understand your attachment style and what sets you off, you can learn how to communicate your needs and wants to your partner without becoming overly sensitive.

Communication is key to the success of any relationship, and once you understand why you love the way that you do, you will be able to better communicate with your partner.

IN SEARCH OF THE SECURE PARTNER

If you think that the secure attachment style is well put together, you're right. They understand their relationship and the emotions and connections behind them. This type of attachment style isn't looking for extreme emotionality, but instead they desire to feel an even-keeled, perpetual sense of joy.

Why is the attachment bond important? An attachment bond is an emotional connection between two people.

Fearful-Avoidant in Love

Starting from a young age, the nonverbal connection between mother and infant is deep. The emotional attachment that a child feels with its caretaker is based on the needs that the caretaker provides for the child, which are based on emotions. As crucial as this bond is, it's formed on the mental stability that the child receives for the caretaker or parent.

These attachments vary based on the needs of the child and support given by the caretaker. Understanding the basic needs that a child has and how to fulfill them is no different than what a relationship partner must do during adulthood.

The lack of support or nurturing causes attachment issues with the caretaker during the development of the child. A happy infant indicates that their needs have been met by the caretaker. This leaves the child with a sense of security and satisfaction. If a child isn't taken care of or made to feel safe or loved, they will form negative attachment styles to their caretaker.

Everything a secure partner does in their relationship makes sense because they clearly understand the ups and downs of the relationship. This type of partner sees the benefit of fighting through pain. Hardship means nothing to them because they use it to make their relationship stronger. If your partner is this type of attachment style, then you've seen how empathetic, concerned, and patient they are with those they love.

If you need someone to talk to, they are your person since they make great listeners. This type of partner thrives when things aren't good. With an accepting attitude, they appreciate their love ones the way they are, and they never try to change them or make them into something they're not. This type of partner is a good one to have. This type of attachment style partner wastes no time acknowledging their emotions or validating their feelings.

They simply get it. They are looked at by their families as an emotional coach. Talking things through in order to get to fix the problem it is what they do. The secure attachment style partner isn't afraid of getting to the bottom of the problem in a relationship. They aren't afraid of finding out the truth, even if it's painful. They are tough, and they understand the process of healing pain and trauma.

If you find that intimacy doesn't come naturally, you must seek to improve that aspect of yourself to make your relationships stronger.

Fearful-Avoidant in Love

Having a healthy relationship is up to you, and you can do so by understanding your attachment style. Knowing this can play a major role in how you view your partner. Fear influences emotions and makes people hide their feelings to avoid getting hurt. It can make you doubt yourself and feel as if you don't deserve to be loved. If you want to stay with your partner but don't know how to develop the intimacy that's needed for a stable connection, you must first look within to get to the root of the issues that plague you.

CHANGE YOUR ATTACHMENT STYLE

We all form some kind of attachment in life, whether it's beneficial or not. From the time we're young, attachments are a part of life. How we attached to our mother or caretaker sets the stage for what we want and expect in our relationships.

The absence of positive attachments can upset people and cause them to experience a variety of negative emotions. If you don't like how your relationship is playing out, it's never too late to change your attachment style now that you're aware of your behavior and thinking patterns. If you want to be more open, loving, and trusting you must open your heart and refuse to fear love and intimacy. To let go of attachments, you should let go of negative thinking which leads to behaviors that cause pain, sadness, resentment, abandonment, and anger. You should never live your life in fear. When you hold on to possessions and people, the fear of letting go kills you from the inside.

Below is a list of methods that will help you let go of attachments:

- Acceptance – Learn to accept others for who they are, despite how they make you feel.

- Interdependence – Awareness that we're all connected eliminates the fear of entering relationships and expressing your feelings.

- Meditation – Take time to be still and turn off the five senses. This helps your mind focus on the important things.

- Understanding – Being understanding lets your partner know that you care about them.

Healing yourself and correcting your viewpoint on relationships can assist you with letting go of the fear of making connections. Allow your relationship to grow by removing fear from the equation.

Below is a list of ways to improve your thinking:

- Be honest and straight forwarded.
- Be more assertive.
- Listen without judgment.
- Love yourself.
- Peacefully resolve conflict.
- View yourself as strong, powerful, and intelligent to improve self- esteem.

If you want your relationship to be healthy, you must take the steps above.

ATTACHMENT STYLES

Your viewpoint of attachments can play a major role in the failure or success of your relationships. There are four attachment styles, and one or multiple may currently be playing a role in your relationship.

A recent study by Cindy Hazan, shows that the four attachment styles consist of secure attachment, avoidant-preoccupied attachment, dismissive-avoidant attachment, and fearful-avoidant attachment. Once you analyze your attachment style, you will learn the answers to the many questions you have

Fearful-Avoidant in Love

about why you think and behave the way you do in relationships. In-depth learning of each attachment style and the turmoil they cause in relationships can help you understand why you behave the way you do and then correct those behaviors to create the loving relationship you desire.

Over recent years, I've witnessed people that I care about fall in and out of love because they were searching for certain needs to be fulfilled, but they didn't communicate those needs with their partner. They took no accountability for their actions, which put the full weight of creating a successful relationship on their partner.

But relationships are a two-way street, and the keys to their success are trust and communication. Therefore, some of my friends experienced failed relationships because one or both of those qualities were missing.

Maybe, you were in a relationship where your partner blamed you for not making them feel happy or loved. This is why understanding attachment styles is so important, because it can give you the clarity that you need to create a successful, long-lasting relationship. Have you been struggling in your relationship? Do you need answers? Do you need constant attention from your partner, and when you don't receive it, do you feel like they don't love you?

The answers you seek are in your attachment style. Don't make your relationship harder than it has to be because you have needs that you haven't made clear, or worse, that you're forcing onto your partner. What you want out of a relationship speaks to your attachments throughout life. Some of us hold on for dear life to our partners, while others seem to take a don't-care approach. Whatever's going on in your relationship should be looked at from the perspective of one of the four attachments styles.

In the next chapter, we will take a closer look at how attachment styles affect our perspective and whether we can love, trust, and feel secure within our relationships. One thing is for sure is that you are not alone. Many people you know are dealing with the same issues to some degree within their relationship.

Relationships either get stronger or fall apart. There is no standing still. Decide which direction you want to move with your partner.

WHAT DO YOU WANT FROM ME?

Allowing others to control your feelings can cause anxiety. This can be seen within the attachment styles. Most people don't just have one attachment style, but several, depending on past relationships.

Gaining an understanding of yourself is as important to the success of any relationship. If you're not careful, you can allow bad breakups of the past to negatively affect your current relationship.

This is the case for many people who date. Have you ever thought about what you really want out of life? Do you see your attachment style affecting your relationships?

Do you feel as if your partner doesn't understand you? Many times, people get involved with people that they think they can change. The truth is, you can only change yourself. Focus on yourself, and as you grow, your experiences will change. Do you give love? Are you having a hard time trusting people? Taking a look in the mirror and evaluating how you interact with your partner is the way for you to take accountability for your behavior.

Loving yourself is another way. If you can't find happiness within, you won't find it with another person. Be aware of your behavior and how you allow your partner to treat you. If you aren't happy, you should take a second look at your relationship. If your partner isn't looking at their behavior, chances are you're both holding on to what feels comfortable, and that's destructive behavior due to negative attachment styles.

How you see others is based on the different attachment styles you've encountered.

Learning to change your attachment style is key to understanding yourself.

Questioning your own behavior isn't only necessary for you to understand yourself, but healthy. How else will you change your attachment style if you don't look at yourself in the mirror. It doesn't matter if you're dealing with your attachment style or someone's else, you need to understand what's happening and why. Letting go of an attachment style isn't easy because that's the way people have approached relationships throughout their entire lives. If you never analyze the problems in your relationship or your partner and their relationship style, you're more likely to continuously repeat the same issues.

Before we continue, let's talk about how people process thoughts, emotions, and behaviors when it comes to attachment styles. What is it about your partner that keeps you with them? Are you afraid to look at the person for who they are? Are you giving more and receiving less in return? If this is you, understanding why you do certain things in your relationship will help you to understand your own needs.

You might even notice that you or your partner may have more than one attachment style. Knowing as much as you can about each attachment style helps you understand the problem areas in your relationship and how to change them. Remember, if your partner doesn't understand why you're insecure, you will continue to have the same problems. Getting to the bottom of why your relationship is developing in a certain way is a major part of eliminating fears that result from your attachment style.

Learn how to invest in yourself and your partner by changing negative behaviors that hinder your relationship from growing. Most relationships that end in divorce, have that result because one or both partners didn't take the time to understand the needs of their partner or their attachment style. If you aren't a good communicator, you won't be able to express your needs and how you feel. Also, your fear of abandonment due to your attachment style may be keeping you from seeking answers to problems in your relationship. Communicate with your partner daily if you want your relationship to be strong and shed the attachment style that forces you and your partner to sleep with your backs turned.

CHANGE YOUR ATTITUDE

Now knowing that attachment styles can cause more harm than good, you should work even harder to change yourself or help your partner understand what's going wrong in your relationship. Refusing to work on your relationship isn't going to magically make things improve. Your relationship will only get worse.

Attachments include emotional bonds. Many people deal with self-esteem issues and struggle to understand what they need to do to experience security and happiness. Getting out of your head to focus on a better relationship isn't easy for some people. Many couples have found that expressing their true feelings isn't always safe. No one wants their fears to be used against them, but this occurs in some relationships. Having attachment styles in your relationship that cause issues such as low self-esteem, fear, anxiety, and trust issues can be dealt with the right way.

Relationships aren't easy. It takes working together and understanding your partner's needs for them to be successful. People can feel when they're not being valued in a relationship, so you should be sure to show your partner how important they are to you. How much of your relationship problems can be traced back to childhood or broken relationships of the past? Unhappy people have some of the worst attitudes, and poor attitudes that lead to even more issues that destroy the core of any relationship.

Below is a list of what you can do to change your attitude and improve your relationship:

- Accountability – Take responsibility for the role you've played in your relationship.

- Develop intimacy – Emotional closeness builds a healthy connection. You won't experience intimacy if you refuse to let each other in.

- Eliminate fear – When working on your relationship, you will have moments of fear and anxiety, but don't let that stop you. Continue to press forward.

- Forgive – Forgive your partner for times they've hurt you in the past and forgive yourself for your hurtful actions.

- Honesty – Share your feelings and don't hold back. For things to change, you must tell the truth.

- Let go – Stop bringing up the past.

You can't move forward if you keep looking backward.

- Speak up – Speak what's on your mind but watch your tone and how you say things. Letting your partner know what hurts you is healthy but also be opened-minded to how the other person feels.

A positive attitude brings sunshine to any situation. If you don't fight for your relationship, no one else will. Don't let past attachment issues that stem from your childhood, hurt your current relationship. If your mother neglected you as a child, it doesn't mean your partner will do the same thing. Be willing to trust your feelings as well as see the good in your partner, even if you're afraid. In time, your relationship will move into a healthier state without either of you having to force it. Correcting your mindset is also the key to working through attachment style conflicts. The more you improve mentally, the strong your relationship will become.

Below is a list of ways to improve your relationship:

- Be open-minded.
- Don't stress over little things.
- Know yourself and love yourself.
- Learn to trust your partner by sharing your fears.

- Listen without judgement.
- Show your partner how much you love them daily.
- Speak positive words to each other. Think positive thoughts about each other.
- Take accountability for your thoughts and actions.
- Talk about the things that matter to both of you.

A strong, healthy relationship takes working together. If you aren't willing to work together for the health of your relationship, you aren't willing to give your best. Going forward, make your relationship the number one priority in your life.

Vulnerability and intimacy sparks change

Vulnerability and intimacy can spark change. Many couples with attachment issues will argue about the wrong things and getting to the core issues in the relationship can be a battle. What's really going on?

How can you stop negative feelings and move towards positive change? Learn how to give more of yourself. This is the key to anything. Don't just say things that sound good. You should do things that prove your love and loyalty to your partner.

Many of the underlying issues in relationships have more to do with someone not being able to express their feelings in a non-defensive way.

Keeping things bottled up inside isn't beneficial. Talking about the real issues begins the process toward overcoming those problems. The more you talk about your problems without attacking each other, the deeper your connection becomes. One way of knowing that you're both growing is by measuring how much you open yourselves to vulnerability. You simply can't have intimacy without vulnerability.

Sharing what's in your heart sparks intimacy. Change starts with you. If you're spending your time questioning your partner's behavior, you're on the wrong track. Words have a huge impact on others.

Sometimes more than actions. Stop blaming your partner for what they didn't do right in the past. Stop putting each other down for the sake of hurting each other. Change starts with you. Let go of the resentment you feel towards your partner or you will have a hard time changing yourself. Unforgiveness is a major reason for your war-torn relationship that's filled with anger. Decide to change that today.

How you consistently treat each other has much to do with your connection. If you understand your partner and yourself, you will better understand what you need to do to make the relationship work.

Staying together when you both have multiple attachments styles will take some work. Are you willing to work on your relationship?

Are you willing to forgive yourself and your partner? Do you see your relationship working despite the attachment styles? Can you see past negative behaviors and work together?

If you can see the positive in a negative situation, you have a fighting chance in making your relationship work. Remember, there's no one to change but self. Stop pointing the finger and improve you thought patterns. Only then will you notice a change in everything and everyone around you.

- Let go of the pain from the past – Holding on is only destroying you and your relationship.

- Remember why you fell in love – This is often overlooked when there are problems in relationships. What was it about your partner that made you want to be with them initially? If you can answer this, you have a fighting chance.

- Take a vacation together – When was the last time you guys took a trip to rekindle your relationship?

Getting rid of negative attachment styles that hold your relationship hostage should be something you start doing immediately. It should be something you want to do for the health of your relationship. It only takes self-improvement and getting out of your own way to create change.

HOW ATTACHMENT STYLES CAN AFFECT YOUR RELATIONSHIP

If you've been in a relationship where your partner wasn't emotionally available, you know how awful that can feel. Yes, negative attachment styles can affect the success of any relationship. And to make matters worse, you can become exhausted from attempting to work things out. You've been down this road more times than you can count, and you're now questioning whether it's even worth fixing anymore.

You must be present in order to change what is taking place in your relationship. It isn't going to simply fix itself. If no one is willing to talk about the problems, chances are you all are emotionally disconnected from each other. Now may be the time to fix yourself so you can tackle the true issues plaguing your relationship.

Attacking your partner's attachment style isn't the answer. And forcing others to take sides and stack blame on you partner doesn't work either. Your attachment style has crippled the relationship, and neither one of you are willing to admit this truth or evaluate your heart. Your success is based on what you're willing to change to save your relationship.

Below is a list of things that may trigger the hurt you carry around that was caused by past relationships.

- Dismissive and distance attitude.
- Lack of communication.
- Lack of concern for your feelings.
- Neglectful and detached behavior.

If you want to eliminate the negative attachment styles that exist in your relationship so that you and your partner can have the success you desire, be willing to open up and share your feelings. Communication is the key. In the end, your relationship should be worth fighting for.

Below is actions you can take to have success in your relationship:

- Confront your fears. Understand that you can't have a healthy relationship if you're not willing to admit your attachment style and fix it.
- Stop blaming your partner for everything and take a close look at yourself.
- Identify the problems within yourself and stop worrying about your partner's issues.

- Set limits on what you're willing to accept.

Any form of success takes hard work and dedication. If you aren't dedicated to creating a successful environment and a happy union, your neglect is destined to destroy everything you've worked so hard to build.

CONCLUSION

When it comes to relationships, the foundation is set during childhood and will continues to influence your behavior throughout adulthood if you don't consciously decide to change that. Your childhood influences can play a major role in the success or failure of a relationship.

Knowing how you feel about relationships and why you feel that way can help you understand your needs and your partner's needs as well. I will continue to break down the four different attachment styles for those seeking to understand the needs of the relationship, themselves and their partner.

What could have taken place during your partner's development stages that causes them to hold on tight to the relationship and constantly seek validation and approval from you? Because of lack of understanding, they can't move past crisis in your relationship.

Talking about your partner in a negative manner isn't going to fix the damage to your relationship. You must be willing to evaluate your own attachment issues. If love is what you want, don't run from it, and don't sabotage the time and hard work you've put in.

Improvement in your relationship will take time, but it can be worked out. Taking a step back to evaluate what has gone wrong and how it can be fixed, will only help your relationship. Knowing what your attachment style is helps you to identify the problems that have been affecting your relationship.

Deeply rooted attachment issues hinder relationships from flourishing. You don't have to accept the fear of love and intimacy. Since you now know and understand your

Fearful-Avoidant in Love

attachment style, you can begin to think and behave in new ways. If you want to have a deeper connection with the person you love, begin the self-improvement process.

It's your responsibility to change yourself, not your partner. It's also your responsibility to love yourself, so that you're able to give and receive love. Stop putting your unwarranted attachments and fears in front of your relationship, and I guarantee you will have a much stronger bond with your partner.

If you want to have a successful relationship, learn what's keeping you and your partner from having a deep and meaningful connection. If you're not able to make the necessary changes on your own, find a relationship counselor who can help shed light on what's causing the emotional blockage in your relationship.

Once you understand each other's needs, fears, and desires, your relationship will begin to flourish. Communication is the key. If after reading this book you still have questions about your relationship, feel free to reach out to me via my email address johannasparrow44@gmail.com for a session. Please know that I do charge $45.00 for a one-hour phone session.

Fearful-Avoidant in Love

Made in the USA
Monee, IL
21 May 2023